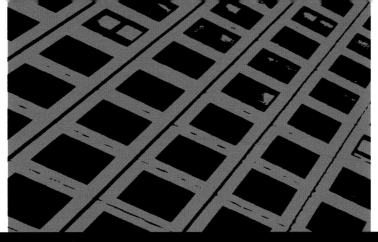

Can You Guess What I Am?
In the Street

J.P. Percy

W
FRANKLIN WATTS
LONDON • SYDNEY

How to use this book

This book combines the fun of a guessing game with some simple information about familiar sights on the street.

Start by guessing
- Carefully study the picture on the right-hand page.
- Decide what you think it might be, using both the picture and the clue.
- Turn the page and find out if you are right.

Don't stop there
- Read the extra information about the animal or object on the following page.
- Turn the page back – did you miss some interesting details?

Enjoy guessing and learning
- Don't worry if you guess wrong – everyone does sometimes.
- Your 'guessing' will get better the more you learn.

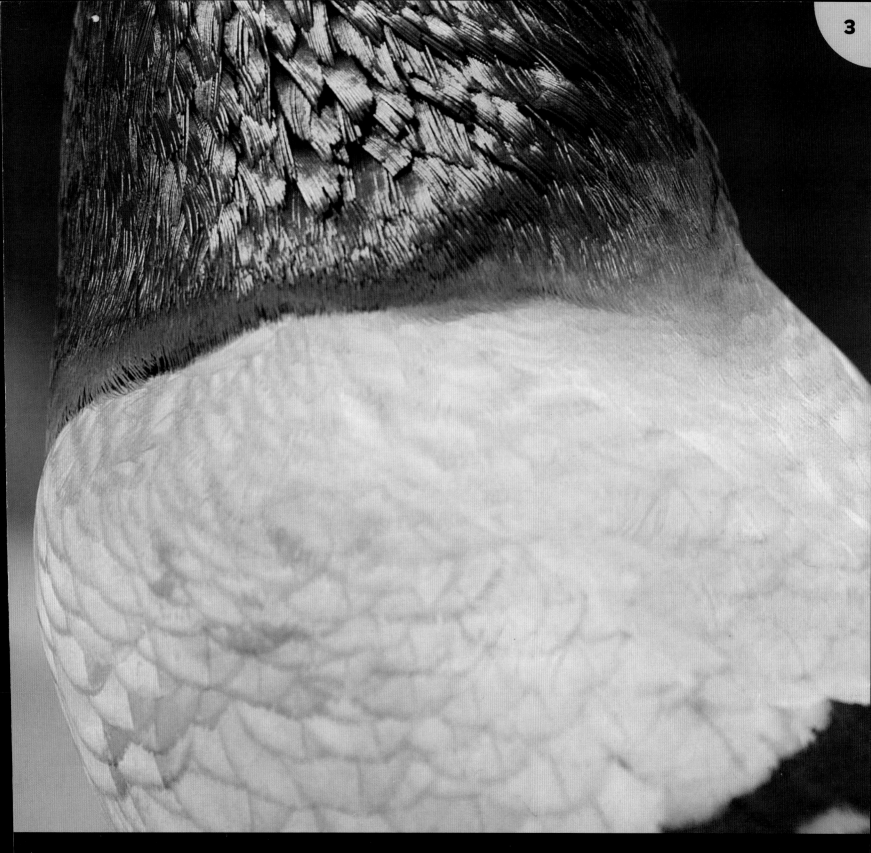

I eat crumbs and I have feathers. Can you guess what I am?

I am a Pigeon!

Many types of pigeon live in towns and cities. In some places, there are so many pigeons that people use birds of prey – such as hawks – to scare the pigeons away.

I go up when it is wet. Can you guess what I am?

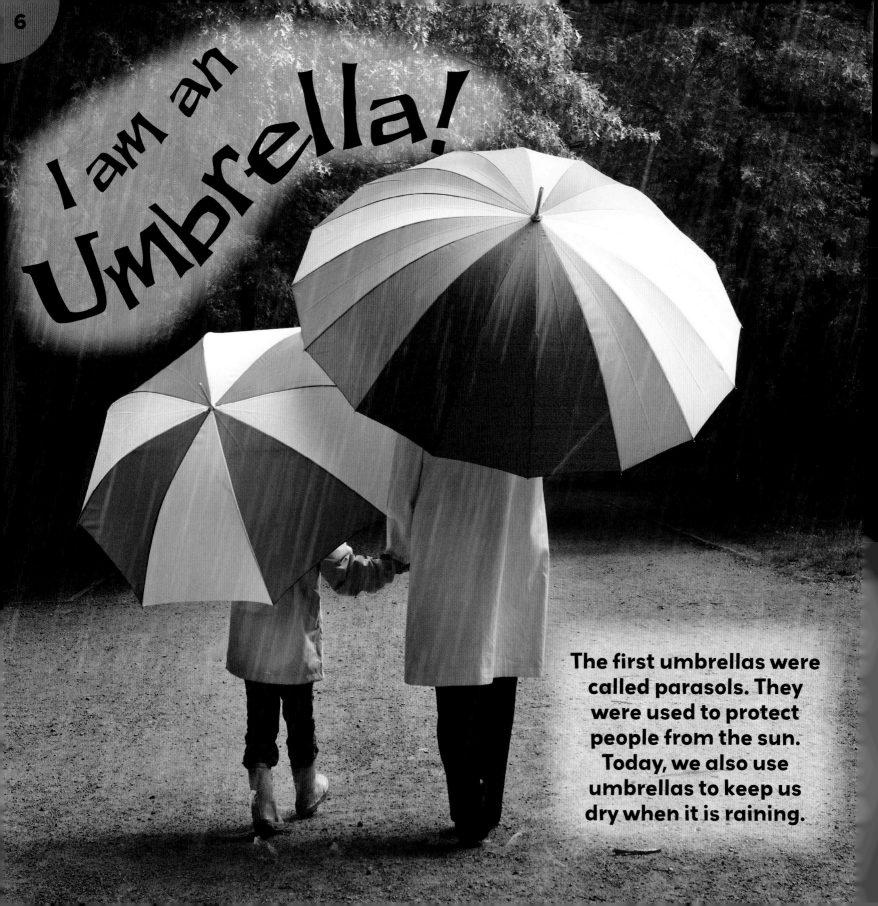

I am an Umbrella!

The first umbrellas were called parasols. They were used to protect people from the sun. Today, we also use umbrellas to keep us dry when it is raining.

I tell you when to stop or go. Can you guess what I am?

I am a Traffic Light!

Traffic lights have red, amber and green lights. They tell the traffic when to stop and go. Traffic lights help cars and trucks to drive safely on the street.

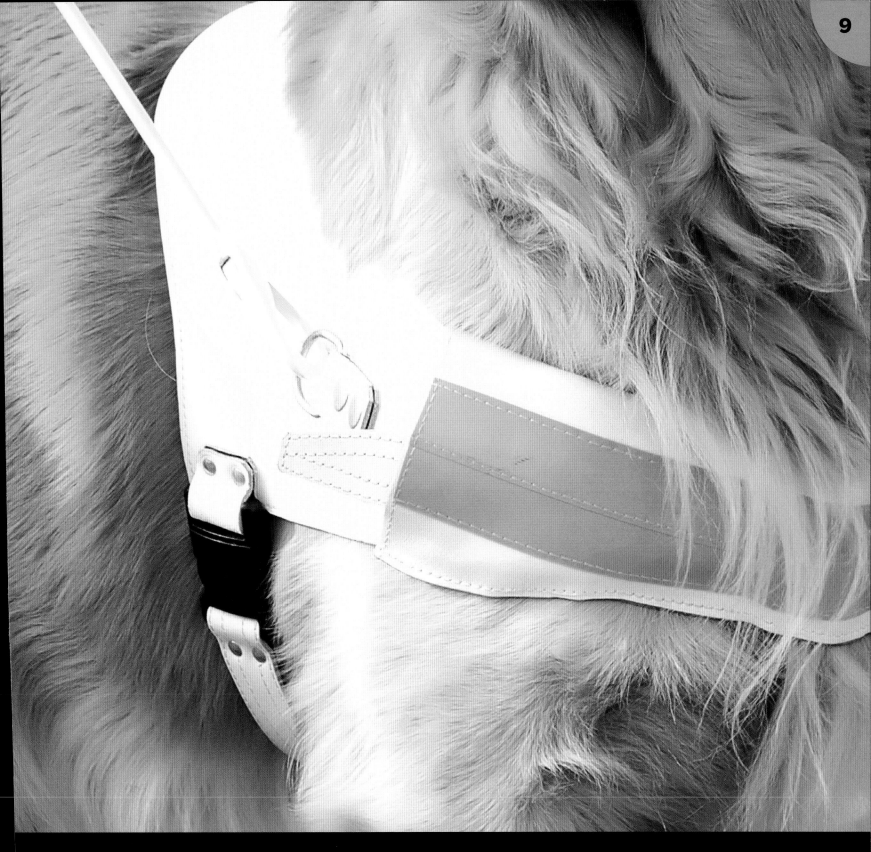

I have four paws and I help my owner. Can you guess what I am?

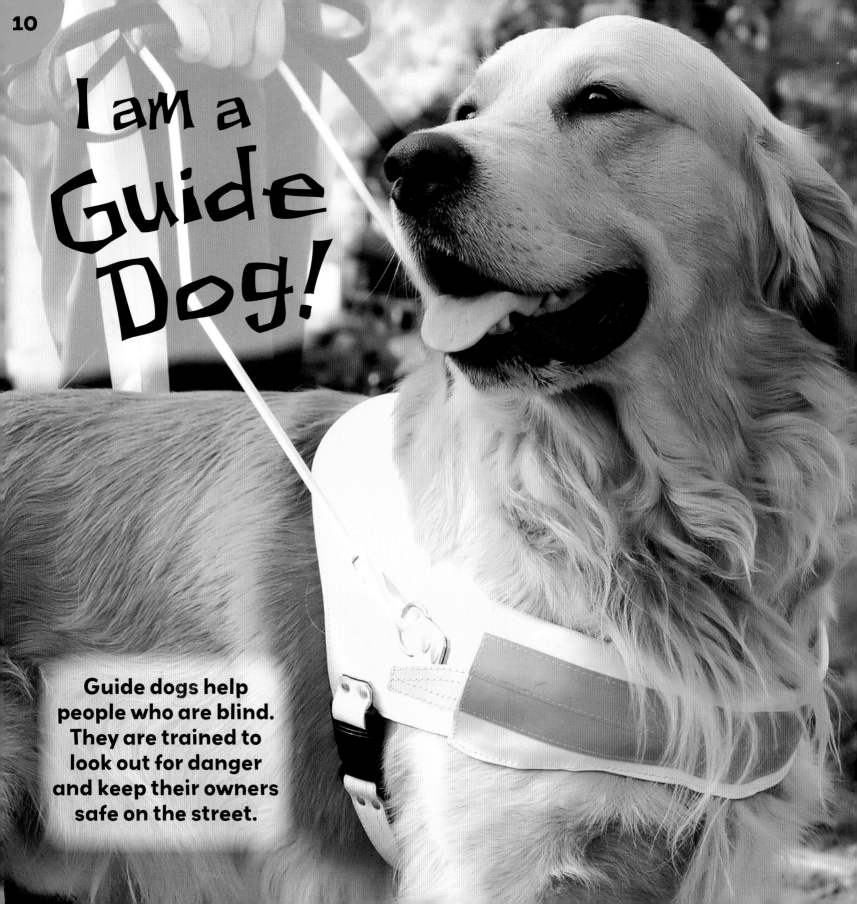

I am a Guide Dog!

Guide dogs help people who are blind. They are trained to look out for danger and keep their owners safe on the street.

11

Riding me on the street is a lot of fun. Can you guess what I am?

I am a Bicycle!

Bicycles are a fun way to get around. The harder you push the pedals the faster you can go.

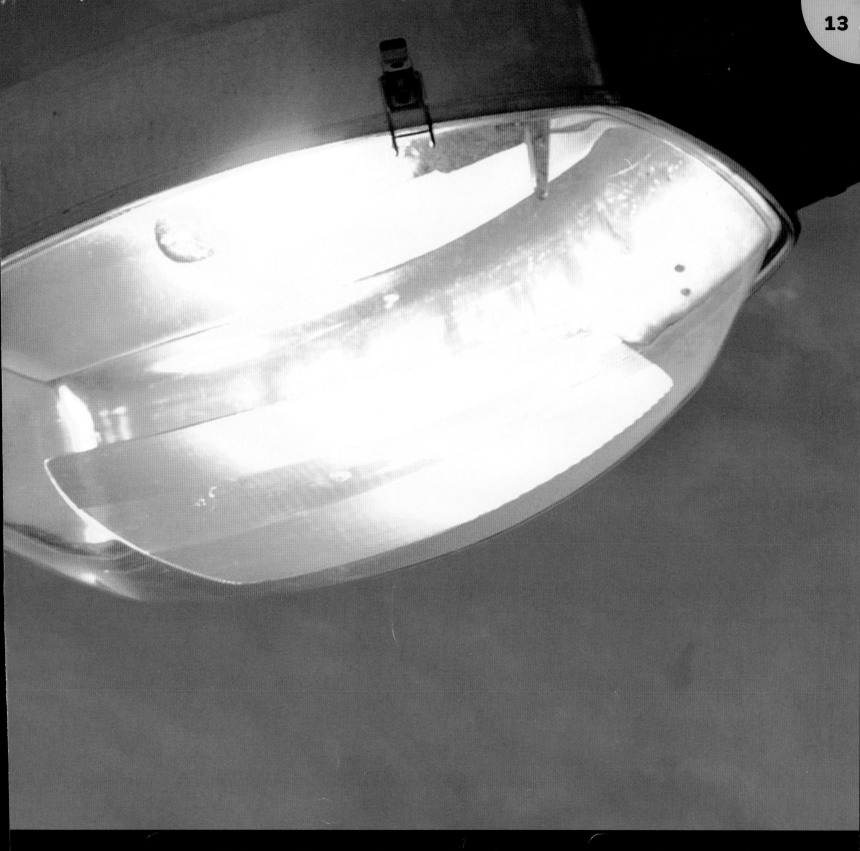

I go on at night and go out in the day. Can you guess what I am?

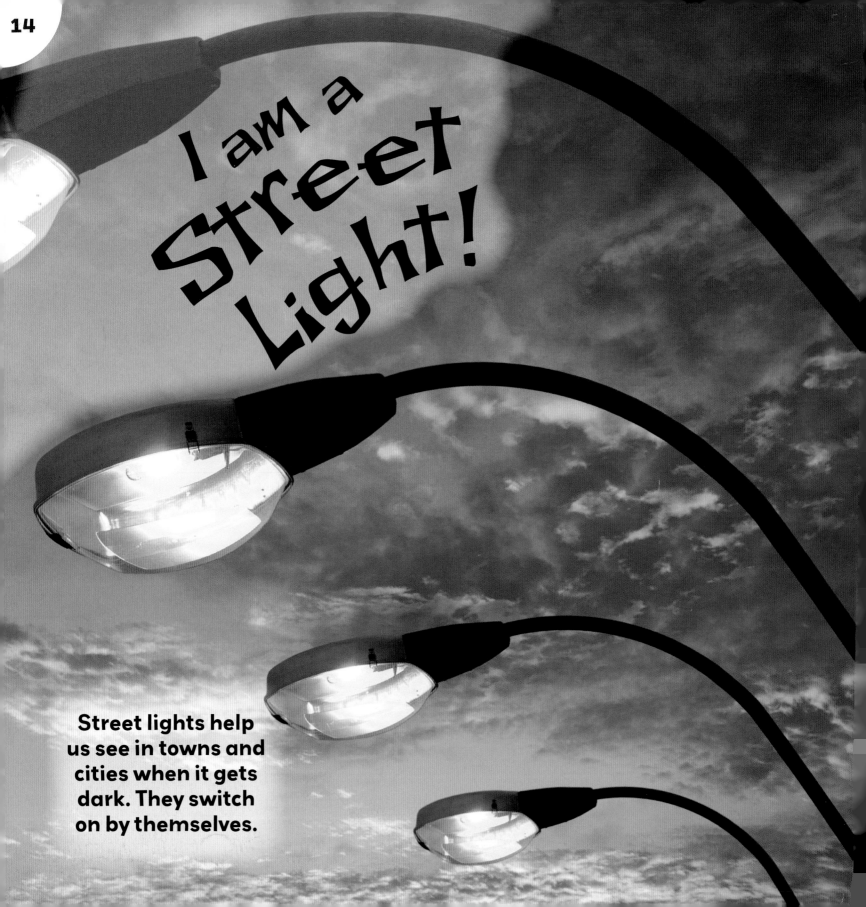

I am a Street Light!

Street lights help us see in towns and cities when it gets dark. They switch on by themselves.

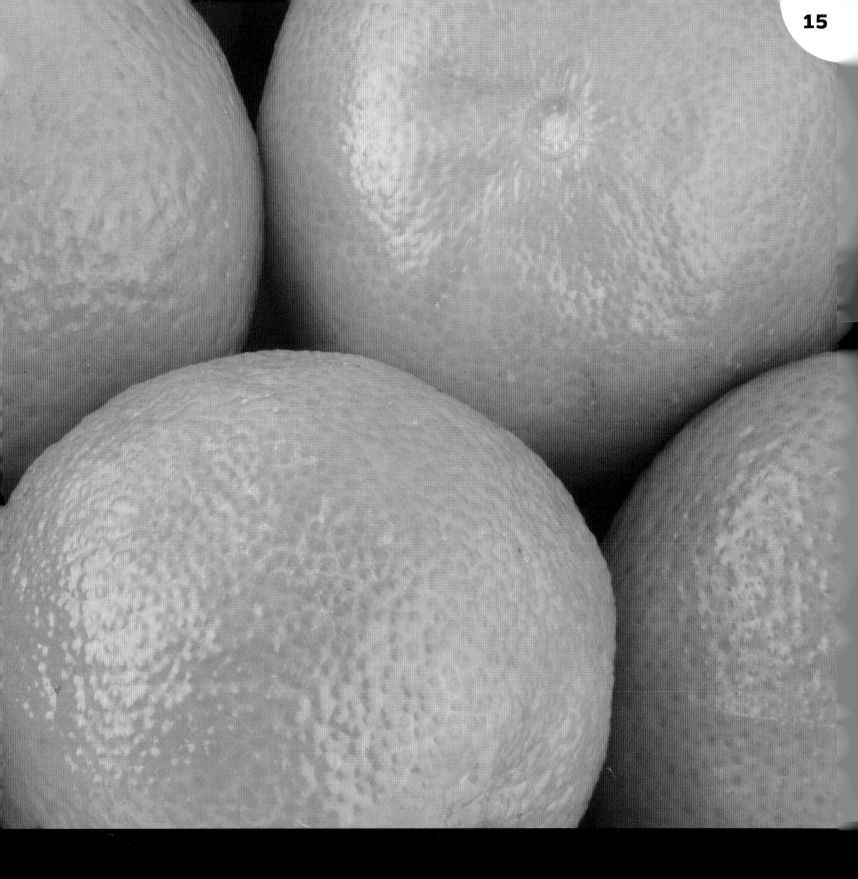

I am a Market Stall!

Market stalls are a good place to buy lots of fresh fruit and vegetables. They are very noisy places – the market-traders shout loudly to tell you what they have for sale.

I move heavy things from place to place. Can you guess what I am?

I am a Truck!

Today we use trucks to move big things around. A hundred years ago, we used horses and carts to do the same jobs.

I am noisy and full of people. Can you guess what I am?

I am a Carnival!

Steet carnivals and parades
are fun ways to celebrate.
People dress up in colourful
costumes, play music and sing
and dance along the street.

Now try this...

Think it!
The next time you are in the street, imagine you are a guide dog. What does a guide dog need to stay away from to keep their owner safe?
Talk about what is dangerous in the street. What can you do to stay safe?

Draw it!
Draw a picture of your favourite vehicle. It could be a car, a truck or a bus.
Draw yourself in the driving seat of your vehicle or stick a small photograph of yourself behind the wheel.

Write it!
Street markets have lots of things to buy. Some stalls sell fruit or vegetables and some sell meat or fish. Think of a meal that you enjoy eating. Write a shopping list of ingredients that you could buy from the market.

First published in 2012 by

Franklin Watts
338 Euston Road
London NW1 3BH

Franklin Watts Australia
Level 17/207 Kent Street
Sydney, NSW 2000

Series editor: Amy Stephenson
Art director: Peter Scoulding

Picture Credits:

Dewey number: 590
ISBN: 978 1 4451 1064 6
Printed in China

Franklin Watts is a division of Hachette Children's Books,
an Hachette UK company.
www.hachette.co.uk